FIT TO BE TIED

Vintage

TIES

OF THE FORTIES AND EARLY FIFTIES

Photography by John Tenny

I believe everything I've been told about neckties:

1. They satisfy modern man's desire to dress in art. (Really, there are very few RIGHT ways to wear a painting. Painted pants are too much, jackets the same. Hats are nice the way they are, so leave them alone– Socks, who notices? Shoes don't count–they're not really clothes, they're protection–like a bullet proof vest or a rubber. Painted shirts are all right except they don't look good with ties.)

2. There's something spiritual, talisman-like about a necktie. Something you want to hold on to while praying. Like Lou Costello.

3. I will someday get mine caught in a sheet metal machine and die horribly.

I love my ties, partly out of respect, partly out of fear.

SINCERELY

Harry Anderson

Harry Anderson–Magician, actor, lover of ties.

FIT TO BE TIED

Vintage

TIES

OF THE FORTIES AND EARLY FIFTIES

By Rod Dyer & Ron Spark

Photography By Steve Sakai

Abbeville Press • Publishers • New York

Editor: Walton Rawls
Designer: Rod Dyer
Production Supervisor: Hope Koturo
Library of Congress Cataloging in Publication Data
Dyer, Rod. Fit to be Tied.   I. Neckties—History.
2. Neckties—Pictorial works.   I. Spark, Ronald P., 1941-   .
II. Sakai, Steve.   III. Title.
GT2120.D94 1987   391′.41 87-12597
ISBN O-89659-756-3
Inquiries should be addressed to Abbeville Press, Inc.,
488 Madison Avenue, New York, N.Y. 10022.
Printed and bound in Singapore by Tien Wah Press.
First edition, second printing.

CONTENTS

I Want My Neckties Wild

The books I read and the life I lead are
    sensible, sane and mild.
I like calm hats and I don't wear spats,
    but I want my neckties wild!

Give me a wild tie, brother, one with a cosmic urge!
    A tie that will swear and rip and tear
When I see my old blue serge;
Oh, some will say that a gent's cravat
    should only be seen, not heard,
But I want a tie that'll make men cry
    and render their vision blurred.

Give me a wild tie, brother
One with a lot of sins!
A tie that will blaze
In a hectic gaze,
Down where the vest begins.

OK News, 1946
Kiwanis Club,
Oakland, California

6

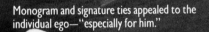

Monogram and signature ties appealed to the individual ego—"especially for him."

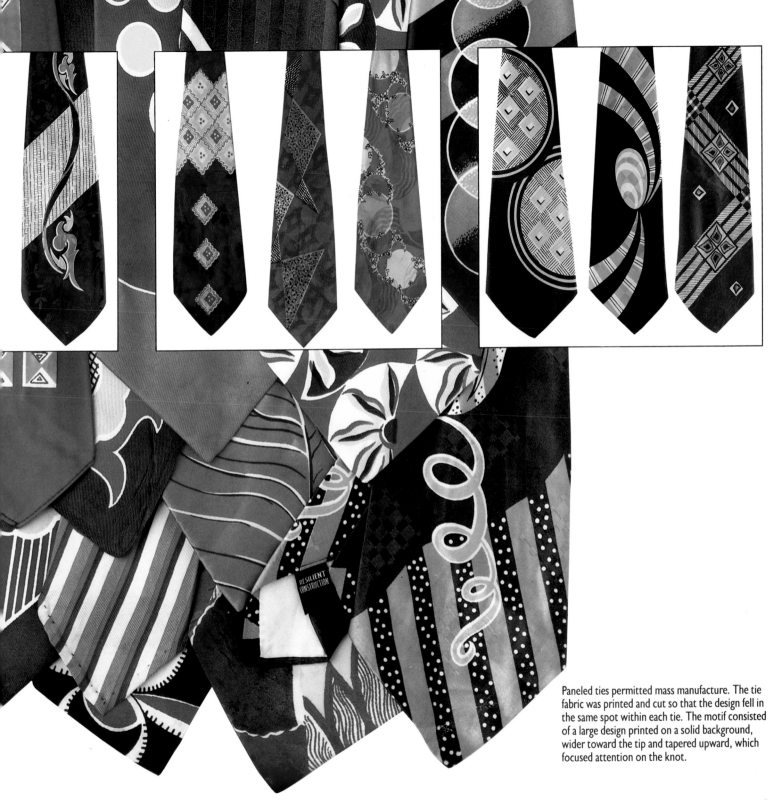

Paneled ties permitted mass manufacture. The tie fabric was printed and cut so that the design fell in the same spot within each tie. The motif consisted of a large design printed on a solid background, wider toward the tip and tapered upward, which focused attention on the knot.

THE TIE-RLESS COLLECTOR

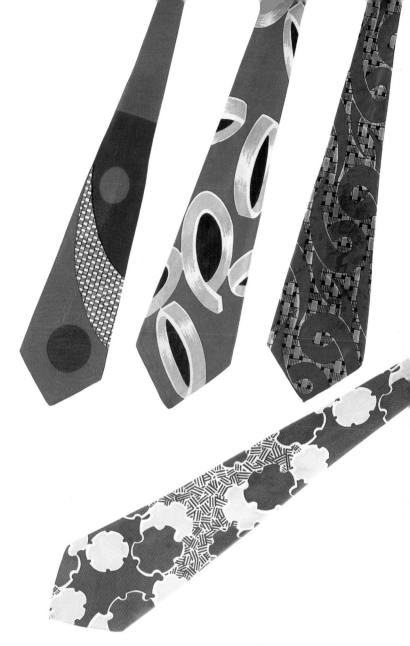

Tell a man you like his necktie and you will see his personality unfold like a flower.

—Countess Mara, 1950

Treasures of wearable art, vintage neckties are just as attractive to me now as they were in the flamboyant years following World War II. My first boyhood memory of '40s neckwear is one of thumbing through *Life* and *The Saturday Evening Post* and being "wowed" by the sharp ties worn by smooth-looking guys in the ads.

I have always been a collector—stamps, baseball cards, tin soldiers (you name it!)— and my childhood bedroom was impenetrable to adults because of the mounds of ongoing collections. Much later, I started collecting neckties, which were readily available, inexpensive, easily storable, and even functional. They served an important need for personal expression, because since entering medical school I've been confined daily to a colorless lab coat. My necktie has become the best and most acceptable way of expressing my personal identity and point of view. For any collector, public recognition is always satisfying, and there is nothing more exciting than to hear "That's a great tie!"

Most collectors enjoy the thrill of the hunt and the discovery of hidden treasure. I always look forward to making the next expedition, but constantly fear that someone has beaten me to El Dorado. On some days I will buy all the ties I can get my hands on (especially if I am unsupervised). On other days, I seem to be restrained by memories of limited budgets, when the choice was lunch *or* treasure. My haunts in those days (and even today) were secondhand clothing stores, flea markets, garage sales, and, now, vintage clothing stores.

It takes about three years, wearing a different tie every day, to go through my collection, and I still get excited by starting the day with the rediscovery of a good old friend. It's not unusual, however, to notice something I hadn't appreciated before: the label, the pattern of·the brocade, or some subtle color or design relationship. Once a tie is selected from the racks crammed into my closet, the rest of my work attire is medically prescribed. After I put my tie on, I feel ready to face the world. I am fit to be tied!

"A tie as young as you feel! You can almost always (well, *almost* always) guess the age of a man by the kind of tie he wears. Men who are still on the sunny-side of their age are apt to go for the tie of a certain sprightliness."—1950 Arrow tie ad

The narrative ties centered around occupational, avocational, or occasional interests.

Dan Duryea in *The Whip*

Arye Gross in *Soul Man*

Henry Fonda in *You Belong to Me*

Elliot Lawrence
records exclusively on
Columbia Records

18

Humphrey Bogart & Edward G. Robinson in *Key Largo*

Elliot Lawrence, Columbia Records

Alan Ladd

CELEBRI-TIES AND TIE-COONS

Rotarian with his tie collection

Mr. William Horsley making a swap

Guy Lombardo ordered his ties in duplicate, one for in-town, one for on tour. Frank Sinatra's wardrobe boasts five hundred. Sinatra often gives the tie off his neck to croon-crazy friends.

—*Good Housekeeping,* 1946

In the late '40s there were quite a few famous tie collectors, and many were written up in magazines and newspapers of the day. Probably the best-known collector was Sherman Billingsley, owner of the Stork Club in New York City, who accumulated no less than three thousand ties, mostly as Christmas gifts. Bandleader Phil Spitalny ("and His All-Girl Orchestra") was right up there with two thousand. One Rotarian made a point of buying a tie in every Rotary community he visited, and his picture in a *Rotarian* article shows him awash in a sea of twelve hundred chest warmers. Mayor William O'Dwyer of New York was especially proud of three pieces from his vast collection: one hand-painted gem sported a lobster holding a phone, another featured galloping giraffes, and the third was a surrealistic beauty with soft, melting watches. Danny Kaye, also a famous tie collector, modeled one of his favorites on Valentine's Day, a number with red lips and white hearts.

Out of affection and humor, '40s necktie wearers developed nicknames for the more outrageous varieties. A "Ham and Eggs" tie was one upon which sloppy eating wouldn't be noticed, and a "Scrambled Eggs" tie was a meatless version. A "Chest Warmer" was a cardiac stimulant, while a "Belly Warmer" was one of the same ilk that functioned at a lower level. A "Christmas Dog" was a tie that it was much better to give than to receive.

Tie swapping was quite in vogue as a way of passing on unwanted neckwear. Probably the most zealous swapper was a Mr. William Horsley, who by 1948 had exchanged more than five hundred ties with other men. Some of these exchanges occurred with perfect strangers, in the middle of city streets. Other collectors formed tie-swapping clubs where a man could send another member his ten worst ties for exchange, in hopes of improving his collection. One such club boasted more than 3,500 members and in its first six months had transacted 17,000 exchanges. In the same spirit, but with a touch of humanitarianism, ties were collected and sent to postwar Europe as part of America's "relief" effort. There were other ways to unload unwanted ties. In fact, a common sales promotion would permit a rebate on disfavored ties that would go toward the purchase of new neckwear. Some stores even went so far as to display the new trade-ins as delightful curiosities and objects for customer amusement—but only if the former wearer agreed.

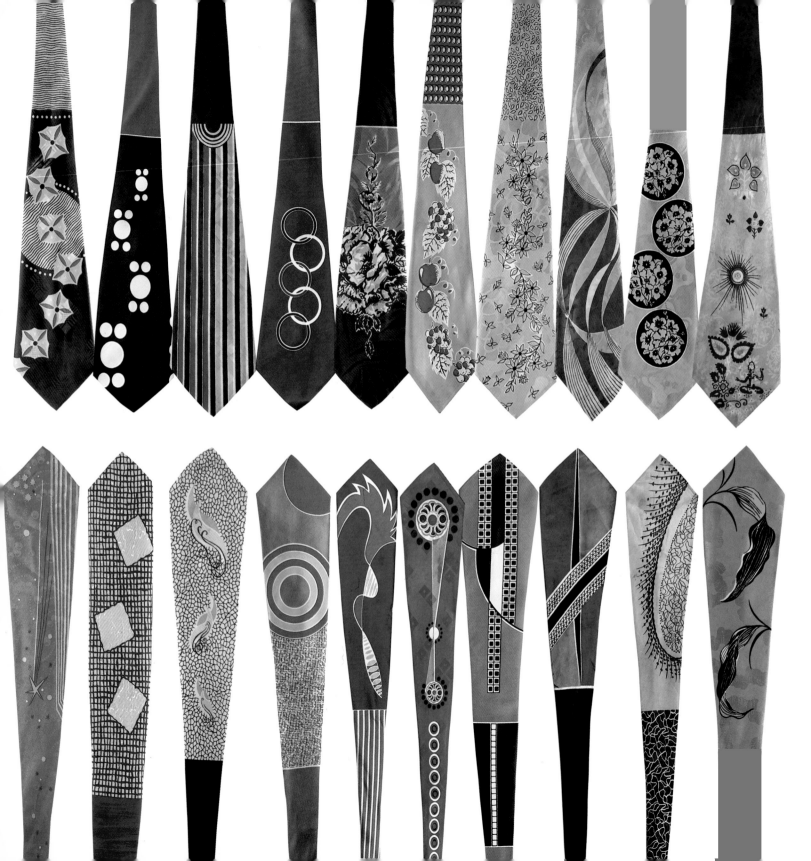

"Knot-planned ties by Hut: the pattern always ties in place."—Hut ad, *Apparel Arts*, January 1945

ETERNAL VERI-TIES

The cravat should not be considered as a mere ornament. It is a criterion by which the rank of the wearer may be distinguished at once and it is of itself a letter of introduction.

—H. Le Blanc, 1829

In contrast to the lineage of other items of wearing apparel, which might date back thousands of years, ancestors of the ornament we now call the necktie stretch back a mere 350 years. In fact, speaking strictly, the modern long tie did not debut until 1860. Of course, there was neckwear before then, but prior to 1636 a man's neck apparel was primarily utilitarian—figuratively or literally. Utilitarian is an accurate description of Roman neckwear. The great orators wore wool-lined neckcloths called *focalia* to guard against hoarseness in cold weather, but Emperor Augustus wore his only at home, fearing that its use in public would be taken as a sign of imperial frailty. Legionaries wore the *sudaria,* a muslin neck wrapping, to absorb perspiration from long marches, and similar scarves and handkerchiefs were used by soldiers everywhere in the next twelve centuries to protect the neck from chafing armor. Only in the seventeenth century does one first encounter a garment that approaches the ornamental function of the necktie: the jabot, a shirt with frilly material cascading down its front.

Most authorities credit Louis XIV with popularizing the forerunner of the necktie, the cravat (from the French *cravate,* meaning Croatian). When a band of Croat mercenaries visited his court in 1636, Louis XIV admired the silk kerchiefs they wrapped around their necks and tied in front. Ever a fashion plate, Louis XIV made the cravat a prestigious ornament of apparel. He appointed a master cravatier, established a light cavalry regiment called the Royal Cravates, and created official silk cravats for his army and navy.

Whatever the origin, it is clear from prints and portraits that the cravat makes its ornamental appearance only about 1650, but the fashion spread quickly. In 1660, Charles II of England brought the style back with him from exile in France. Also in 1660, the first cravat reached America, having been ordered from England, for five pounds, by Governor William Berkeley of Virginia.

In 1692 a surprise attack by the English on French encampments at Steinkirk led to a new fashion in wearing the cravat. In haste, the French officers loosely wound the cloth around their necks and drew the ends through the upper buttonholes of their jackets. Their victory and triumphant return to Paris sparked the tying of the cravat "à la Steinkerque." In later French courts the cravat, in either black or white, was tied low on the neck and had frilly ends, but it underwent dramatic changes during the French Revolution. The citizens of the Republic wore large, highly colored neckties to proclaim their political allegiance.

The first half of the nineteenth century was the golden age of the cravat. In addition to a profusion of fabric colors to choose from, there were at least a hundred recognized knots, including the Gordian Knot, which was so complicated that the wearer could only be extricated by cutting the cravat from his neck. French fashion writer H. Le Blanc even offered a sixteen-lesson course on how to tie the cravat. Beau Brummell,

a famous English dandy, is said to have spent six hours at a time fashioning the folds and bows of his knots. Understandably, to tamper with another's tie was an invitation to a duel.

It was only following the American Civil War that the forerunner of the modern tie, the string tie, appears. The ascot was popular in the Victorian era, and the bow tie and the four-in-hand first became popular in the 1880s. The term "four-in-hand" refers to the knot used by a coach driver to control the reins of a four-horse team. It was also the name of a social club in London where dandies liked to be seen sporting their experiments in new fashion. In France a necktie called a *régate* was derived from

How to simplify Life at 8 A.M.!

Got a Blue Suit ?

If so, *nothing* teams with it like the new blue (or grey) Arrow "Tantivy" shirt-tie-handkerchief combination!

NOTE SHIRT — Observe the smart new stripe effect. Note, too, how good-looking that Arrow Collar is! These Arrow products carry many assets, including "Mitoga" shaped-to-*your*-shape and the Sanforized label. (Fabric shrinkage held to 1%.) $3.95.

Got a Brown Suit ?

If "yes," point it up with a green (*or* tan) "Tantivy Stripes" ensemble! *Depend on Arrow for faultless color combinations!*

NOTE TIE — Chosen by our man (above) is one of the Arrow "Tantivy" group—designed ESPECIALLY for the shirts! Other selections are equally fitting. $1.50.

Got a Grey Suit ?

If so, set it off with Arrow "Tantivy" Stripes" go-togethers—the grey, blue, green, or tan ensembles!

NOTE HANDKERCHIEF — It's an Arrow "Tantivy"—colored to go with the smart "Tantivy" shirt. Perfect! 65¢.

Cluett, Peabody & Co., Inc.

24

Vibrantly colorful designs were achieved by the use of airbrush and dry-brush techniques.

26

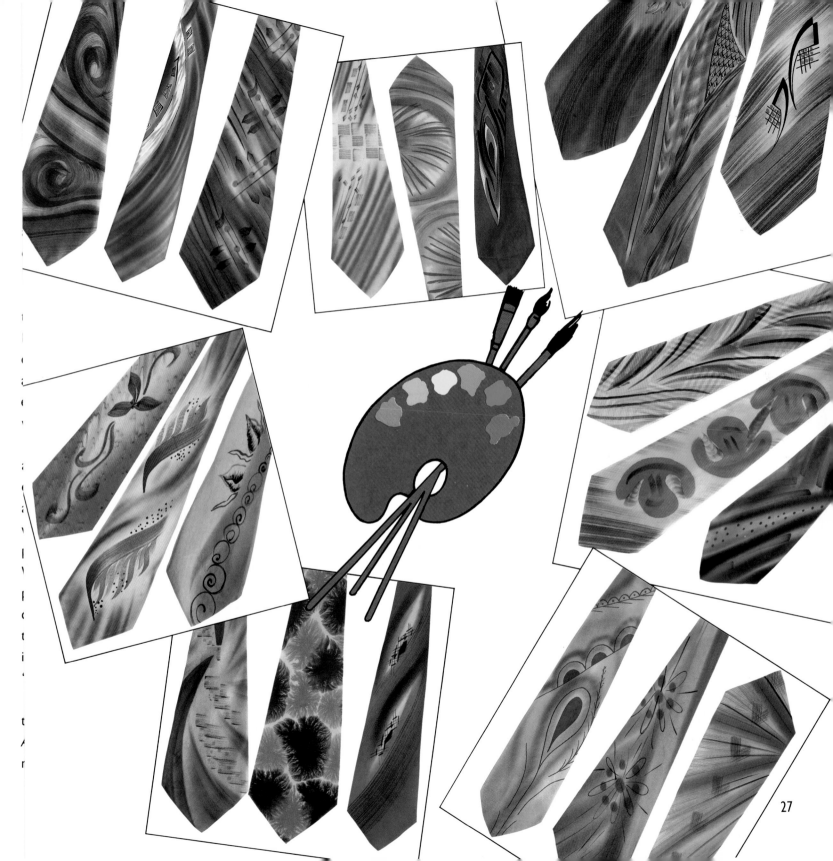

EXPLODED NECKTIE

Diagramatic Drawings
showing construction details

Apparel Arts, February 1946

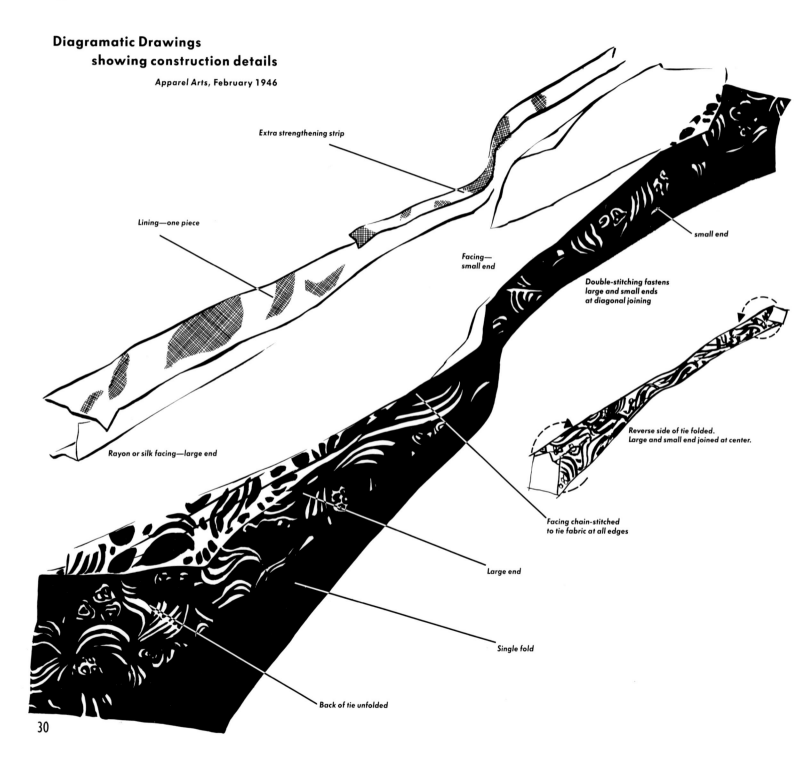

Extra strengthening strip

Lining—one piece

Facing—
small end

small end

Double-stitching fastens
large and small ends
at diagonal joining

Rayon or silk facing—large end

Reverse side of tie folded.
Large and small end joined at center.

Facing chain-stitched
to tie fabric at all edges

Large end

Single fold

Back of tie unfolded

A GOOD QUALITY tie was selected to demonstrate construction of neckwear in this series in which the military technique of "exploding" various pieces of equipment for instruction purposes is applied to various articles of apparel.

Among main points of tie construction is the slip-stitch, running invisibly in the finished tie, from lock-stitch in large end to corresponding lock-stitch at small end. Slip-stitch, hand-drawn in quality ties, requires skilled, experienced workers for proper results. Slip-stitch gives tie added resilience, helps shape and form. Trueness of bias cut is also highly important in tie construction. Accurate 185 degree bias is basis of tie's resilience and makes possible straight drape from knot. Ties cut off bias pull off-center and fall crookedly. APPAREL ARTS thanks Barney Saunders for cooperation in preparing this exploded tie presentation.

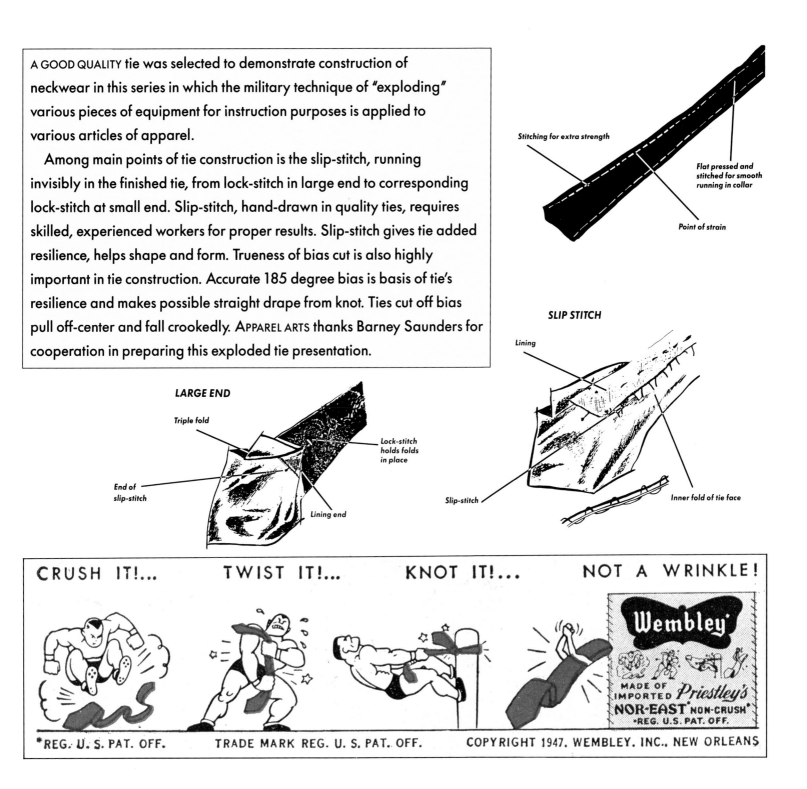

Stitching for extra strength

Flat pressed and stitched for smooth running in collar

Point of strain

SLIP STITCH

Lining

Slip-stitch

Inner fold of tie face

LARGE END

Triple fold

Lock-stitch holds folds in place

End of slip-stitch

Lining end

31

With automatic cutter a New Orleans workman slices cloth into Wembley, Inc. ties. His machine can cut 120 layers.

"Based on the 200 million ties sold in 1950, the raw material used for their construction might have been:

42 million yards of shell fabric
6.25 million yards of lining fabric
10.4 million yards of thread
200 million labels."—Men's Tie Foundation

1 What's a tie? Three pieces of material, wool lining and tape, thread.

2 Cutter in the Van Heusen plant uses glass or plastic pattern, a sharp knife.

Who was making these American creations? In 1946 the Men's Neckwear Manufacturer Association listed more than 600 manufacturers.

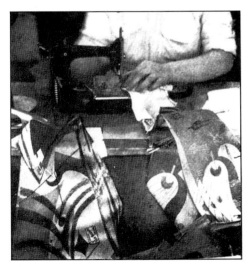

3 Operating: This means sewing in pockets, joining pieces together, turning, pressing.

4 Slip stitching: This is a loose stitch, by hand or machine, that gives tie bounce.

5 The finished product comes in 100,000 color combinations, 40,000 patterns.

A tie priced at $1.50 would be called a "Tie." Under $5.00 a "Cravat." Over $15.00 a "Creation." —1949 tie article

34

THE AMERICAN TIE-IN

Most men like their ties wild today—a reflection, psychologists say, of current world unrest. Tie cycles last from seven to ten years, so it looks like we're in for at least five more gaudy years.

—The Saturday Evening Post, 1946

In late 1943 the suits of American men began to feature wide lapels and padded shoulders and to frame bold neckties. At war for four long years, a devastated Europe could no longer dictate fashion, so the United States set clothing styles for the world with typical flamboyance and optimism. American men needed a psychological lift after a long stretch in GI khaki, and what better way was there to become instantly transformed than to don the latest in bold neckwear? The vivid color combinations and new width were emotionally uplifting. In variety of design, the new ties enabled a man to reflect his individuality, his state of mind, and to evoke memories of pleasurable times, places, and activities.

Optimism was in high gear during the postwar boom in America, and tie manufacturers looked around for graphic design styles that would reflect this exuberance. Without time to create a new design tradition, tie manufacturers quickly reached back for a familiar prewar style, Art Deco. It was a natural and excellent choice, for as a style it had high energy and lively color and exuded a sense of progress that made it a near perfect fit for postwar buoyancy. Over the preceding two decades, art deco-designed items, from locomotives to vacuum cleaners, had grown to be familiar icons of modern living.

Art Deco debuted in 1925 with Le Corbusier's stark, all-white pavilion at the Paris Exposition, where the architect struck a blow against the elaborate ornamentation in artistic design that was highly fashionable at the time. A call for design simplification began to echo throughout Western Europe. The elements of clean surfaces and readable structure were a direct debt to cubism, but these design features were simultaneously reinforced by the architecture and motifs of Egyptian, Aztec, and Mayan antiquities newly uncovered in the 1920s.

In addition to the simplicity of geometric abstract forms, art deco also incorporated stylized floral and organic designs derived from a renewed interest in Japanese prints and textiles as well as the work of Vienna's Arts and Crafts Movement in the '20s. Other common design motifs, such as sunrays, zigzags, and lightning bolts, communicated the sense of speed, progress, and the electrified atmosphere of the Modern Age; they were direct references to American Indian, Babylonian, and African primitive art. Other motifs were stylizations of natural energy symbols, such as the classic art deco leaping gazelle, crouched leopard, and bubbling fountain.

Geometrics: "I like the guys who like 'em bold."
—Gertrude Neisen, 1946 Broadway star

Any man wearing any type of shirt can wear these bold floral ties.

MAGNIFICENT POSSESSION

Beau Brummell Ties

An essential component of art deco is its vivid palette of color and color combinations: lime green, peach, jet black, aqua, chrome orange, cobalt blue, olive, and lavender. Although influenced by oriental and Persian arts and textiles, these color sensibilities are credited to Léon Bakst, designer of the Ballets Russes, and Paul Poiret, fashion czar of '20s Paris. In addition to the forms and motifs of art deco, '40s tie manufacturers also adopted its color spectrum. In fact, the colors and, in particular, the color combinations are immediately recognizable characteristics of the typical '40s tie. An added extension to the art deco color sense is the careful selection by manufacturers of materials for their surface qualities. Mass production, using high-sheen metals and the new synthetic materials, churned out streamlined, glossy products that were both mechanically efficient and comfortable to use. As a direct result, '40s neckties made of rayon and silk have a distinctive smooth surface sheen that acts to visually integrate the streamlined art deco designs and wild color combinations.

The emotional need for release from the tensions of war coincided with the postwar emergence of abstract art and the use of surrealism by com-

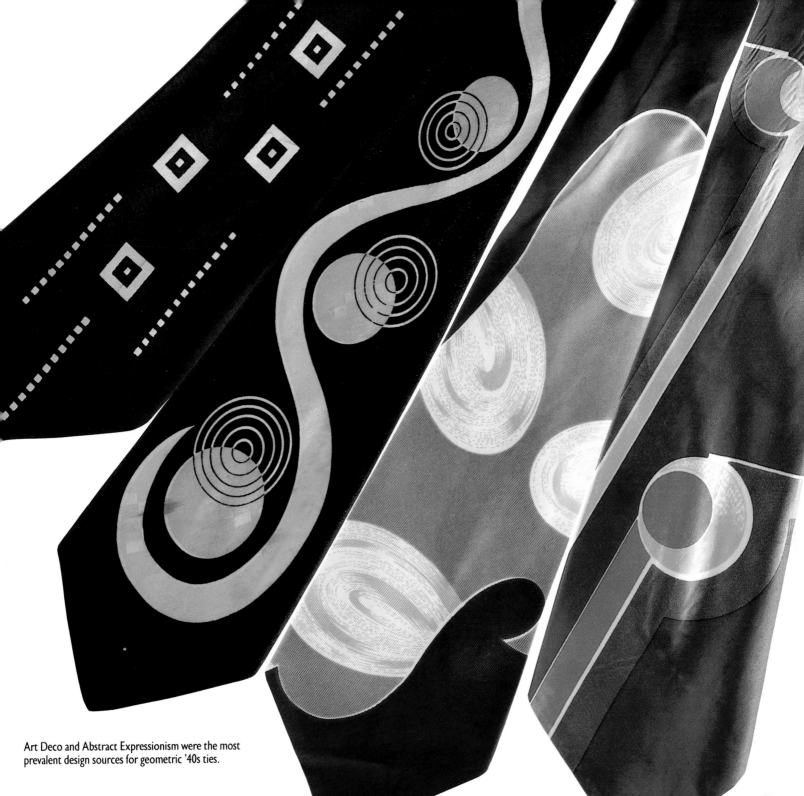

Art Deco and Abstract Expressionism were the most prevalent design sources for geometric '40s ties.

A regular "Gone with the Wind" of the tie business, meaning a runaway seller, was a series of tie designs created by Salvador Dali. There were some problems for tie manufacturer James Lehrer: "Frankly, we had to clean them up a great deal. Bass fiddles with girls crawling out of them, skeletons with pools of blood, may be fine art, but they are not exactly the stuff from which ties are made." Dali did not approve of these revisions.

Salvador Dali, the irrepressible surrealist.

mercial interests. A major contributor to surrealism's public consumption was Salvador Dali, a well-known artist who also designed ties. Both abstract art and surrealism served as immediate tie design material, and especially as a source of kitsch and parody. Bizarre subjects, shapes, and patterns were typical of many '40s neckties. In addition to abstract designs, which were often whimsical if not humorous, many objective designs reflected a return to a man's sense of individuality. Scenes from the Old West, of hunting and fishing, subtle references to past or future vacations on palm-lined beaches, and even ties made of Hawaiian shirt

An obvious Dali influence

Countess Mara produced exclusive ties, usually only fifteen dozen of a kind. She used her initials as a trademark, integrating them into a part of the tie design, and made her customers pay for it. The tie industry referred to this as "name-dropping." But her success induced other tie makers to hire known artists and do the same.

David Crowell, the young ex-marine who became a tie designer, and his daughter Noni. He created many of the neckties put out under the name of Schiaparelli.

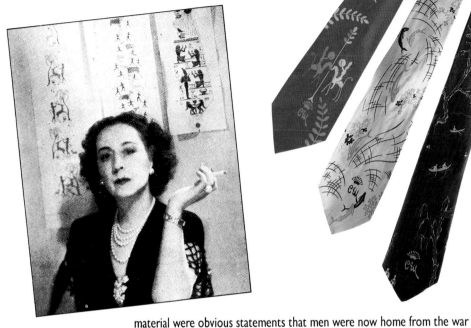

In the fall of 1947, Cheney Brothers introduced a line of pure silk ties with original print designs by Tina Lesser. These limited-edition designer ties had "snob appeal."

material were obvious statements that men were now home from the war and ready to enjoy life's pleasures. There is no greater expression of individuality in the '40s tie than the hand-painted variety, which reached its zenith of popularity during this era. Many hand-painted ties were personalized for the intended recipient. Others depicted a wide range of themes in response to contemporary concerns such as the atomic bomb, flying saucers, television, and, of course, politics.

Finally, there is another very significant design phenomenon of the postwar era: the emergence of women as tie designers. Throughout the '40s tie era, women became famous for designing ties in such important fashion houses as those of Tina Lesser, Elsa Schiaparelli, Countess Mara, and Jacques Fath. In fact, a 1949 *New York Times* article stated that women had become the principal designers of men's ties. How ironic that the majority of '40s men's ties probably were designed by women, made by women, and bought by women.

One of the most popular themes in neckwear.
These ties competed with the actual gamebirds
when it came to colorful fabric plumage.

44

If you were a Cat,
your Tail would Twitch

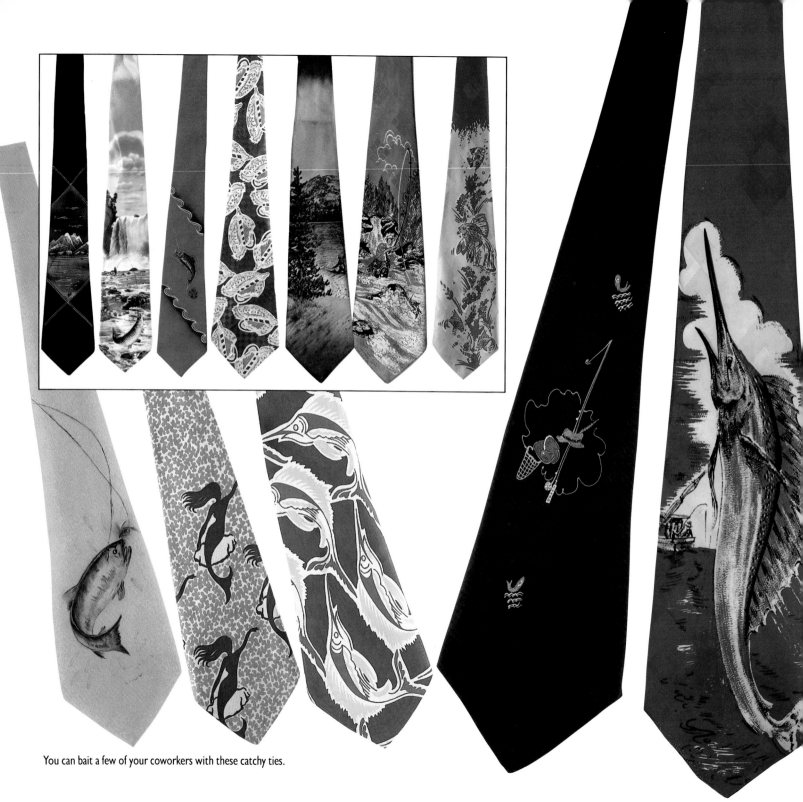

You can bait a few of your coworkers with these catchy ties.

Many a man felt that an exotic bird on the chest was better than two dog ties in the closet.

Ties for sail! Ships and boats galore for all to "sea."

WEAR BETTER

CLEAN BETTER

TIE BETTER

LOOK BETTER

These ties reflect the preoccupation of many a man:
"a hunting we will go."

49

Common tie themes depicted and detailed outdoor scenes. These literally sprouted up in the postwar era.

This could be either man's best friend or a dog of a tie.

Photographic ties debuted in the postwar era. The
technical breakthrough in the fabric printing process
led to their creation.

"To keep pace with the insatiable demand for ties of weird and wild designs, artists have been asked for patterns and themes for handpainted ties."
—Resort and summer menswear article, *Apparel Arts*, July 1944

"Each tie is painted for one man alone—created to complement the personality you plan to please."
—Signet tie ad, *Esquire*, December 1946

The new production method, screen printing, overcame the fabrication bottleneck of hand-blocking tie fabric.

The "Belly Warmer" debuted in 1939 and was made of Hawaiian prints in loud colors. It wasn't until late 1943 that the new neckwear became popular.

54

"Arrow Desert Sands: these Arrow ties are absolutely no mirage!"—Arrow tie ad, *Esquire*, April 1944

The WORLD FAMOUS Cocoanut Grove

CLOSE · COVER · BEFORE · STRIKING

55

"Gay and glorious ties in jungle colors captivate customers and send sales into a heat of activity."
—Smoothie tie ad, *Apparel Arts,* March 1947

"Some like 'em shy, some like 'em neat and some like 'em big and bold! Whatever your dish, Van Heusen has three sizes: small, medium and WOW!"
—Van Heusen ad, *Esquire,* April 1948

WARD
aerials

"The rage for gay ties goes unabated. Printed fabrics dominate as imaginations in many quarters are taxed for motifs."—Tie sales report, *Apparel Arts*, February 1945

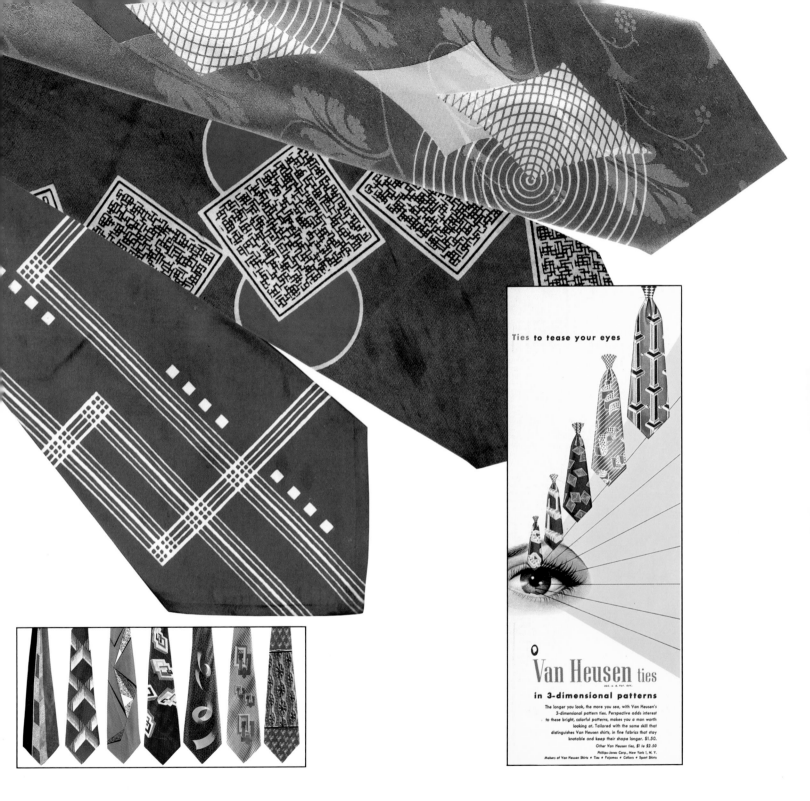

Ties to tease your eyes

Van Heusen ties
REG. U. S. PAT. OFF.

in 3-dimensional patterns

The longer you look, the more you see, with Van Heusen's 3-dimensional pattern ties. Perspective adds interest to these bright, colorful patterns, makes you a man worth looking at. Tailored with the same skill that distinguishes Van Heusen shirts, in fine fabrics that stay knotable and keep their shape longer. $1.50. Other Van Heusen ties, $1 to $2.50

Phillips-Jones Corp., New York 1, N. Y.

Makers of Van Heusen Shirts • Ties • Pajamas • Collars • Sport Shirts

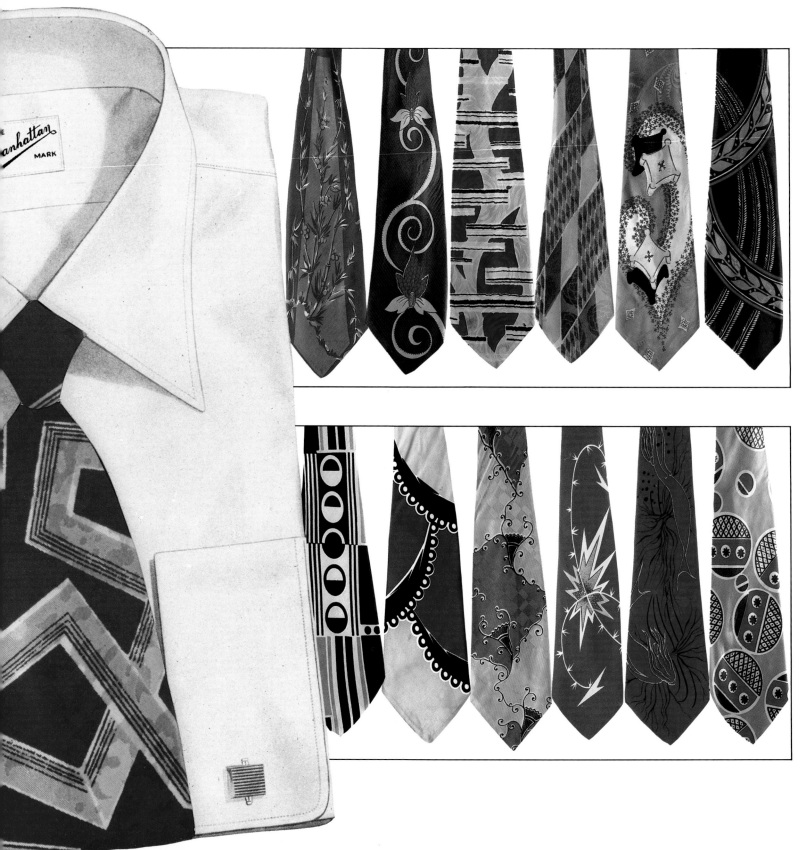

Taking Liber-ties

Color television is here on Van Heusen TV ties. With TV inspired patterns, the gals will focus on channel Y-O-U! Twelve TV patterns—what a reception you'll get!

—*Esquire* tie ad, 1951

The popular culture of the '40s was a major influence on fashion, and fashion influenced popular culture. There was renewed interest in individual expression and nonconformity. One group that gained wide media attention, the Zoot Suiters, was originally perceived as being countercultural. However, the style had a lasting influence on the fashion of the '40s. The zoot suit style is the embodiment of many of the design elements and parody content one sees in the '40s tie. Developed in the late '30s, peaking in 1943, the style was so bizarre that one had to consider it more entertainment than anything else. The costume consisted of voluminous pants, pegged tightly at the ankles, a knee-length jacket with overly broad shoulders, an ankle-length key chain, a broad-brimmed hat, and an oversized bow tie or loud, wide tie.

Movies were a major influence on everything in the '30s and '40s, and the tough guys in gangster films all wore flamboyant neckwear. Many male stars sported bold ties to project a manly image, and one neckwear series called Personali-ties was used to promote individual movie stars, including Bob Hope. Hollywood idols were closely watched, and their clothing was often trendsetting. Alan Ladd and Danny Kaye were featured in tie advertising, and in the late '40s and early '50s television stars also had a strong

Roundup, sombrero, buckaroo...Spirited rodeo themes in mellow California tones. Western ties became popular coincidentally when Western clothing gained a foothold on men's informal wear.

impact. Hopalong Cassidy, the first TV cowboy hero, helped to sell millions of Hoppy outfits to kids and to promote Western duds, including cowboy neckwear, as an informal style for men. As a result, Western themes became popular in tie design, particularly with California tie manufacturers and retailers.

Extremely eye-catching novelty ties with added surface attractions, such as reflective paint, rhinestones, and applied fabric.

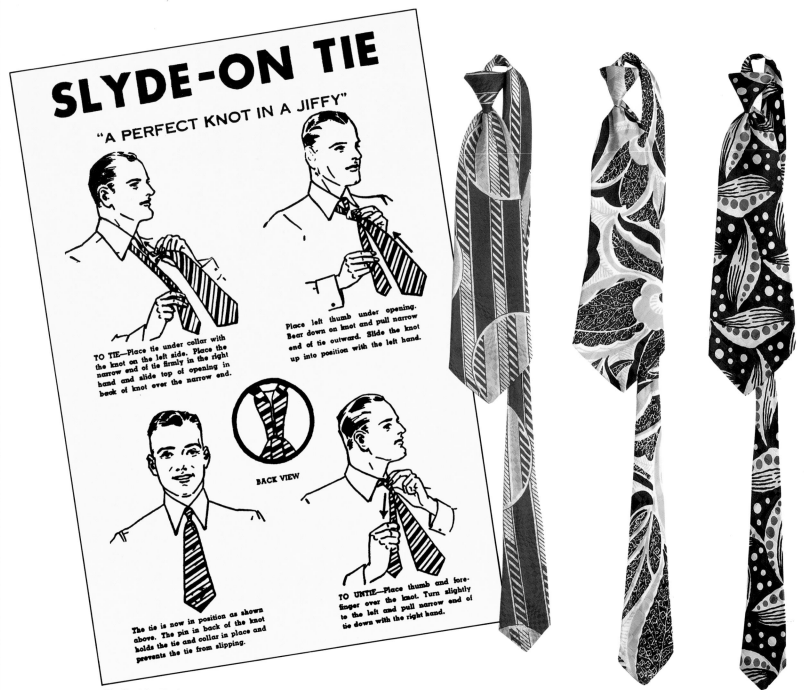

SLYDE-ON TIE

"A PERFECT KNOT IN A JIFFY"

TO TIE—Place tie under collar with the knot on the left side. Place the narrow end of tie firmly in the right hand and slide top of opening in back of knot over the narrow end.

Place left thumb under opening. Bear down on knot and pull narrow end of tie outward. Slide the knot up into position with the left hand.

BACK VIEW

The tie is now in position as shown above. The pin in back of the knot holds the tie and collar in place and prevents the tie from slipping.

TO UNTIE—Place thumb and forefinger over the knot. Turn slightly to the left and pull narrow end of tie down with the right hand.

The Slip-Not Tie Company and the One-in-Hand Tie Company had the lazy man's answer for not tying his tie: the fabricated knot. After crossing the free end under the collar, the tail is pulled through the slot in the back of the knot and positioned in place.

The apron made of ties: no one will ever notice the food spots!

Nance Stilley, 1948 water-ski champion, models the latest in men's neckwear: a twenty-tie, two-piece bathing suit.

Sports figures always had a huge following. The "Bold Look" style, a term coined by *Esquire* in 1948, is apparent in a 1949 *Life* photo of four baseball players in business suits and gaudy neckwear.

Some of the cycles in menswear styles were reflected in women's fashion too. Following four years of wartime scarcities, the typical woman's wardrobe in 1945 consisted of spartan dress suits, skimpy skirts, and unpocketed blouses. Immediately after the war came outrageous styles, including high-heeled shoes (with bizarre ankle straps) and spectacular hats. In fact, a lady in the late '40s never went anywhere without her hat. These millinery creations were very much the equivalent of the man's tie revolution in artistic extravagance and creativity. All this individualistic flair and plumage ended with the "New Look" heralded by Christian Dior's Paris Collection show in 1947. Dior emphasized a restrained, slim, elegant look with a thin waist and a long skirt. The men's equivalent didn't take hold until 1952 when the "Mister T" style promoted a coordinated, restrained clothing ensemble that emphasized a slim contour.

The '40s was also the beginning of the teenage revolution. After stagnant population growth in the '30s, the teenage element in the country shot up by a million in the '40s. These young folks became wage earners and consumers, too, a phenomenon quickly capitalized on by manufacturers. Teenagers enjoyed the "Bold Look" because "Scrambled Eggs" ties had the same irreverence as mismatched shoes and socks, a popular fad of the time. However, tielessness was a growing postwar trend and became a major problem for the industry in the late '40s. To combat it, tie manufacturers did major retail promotions on holiday, seasonal wear, and back-to-school themes. Even a "Good Grooming League" was established by the Men's Tie Institute to "do an educational job on high school boys." It was "all for knot." Informality in menswear grew, and the tie industry never saw a boom like the years 1946 to 1948 again.

"Color symphonies in forty patterns tuned to
the tempo of the times."
—Staple Neckwear, *Esquire*, January 1945

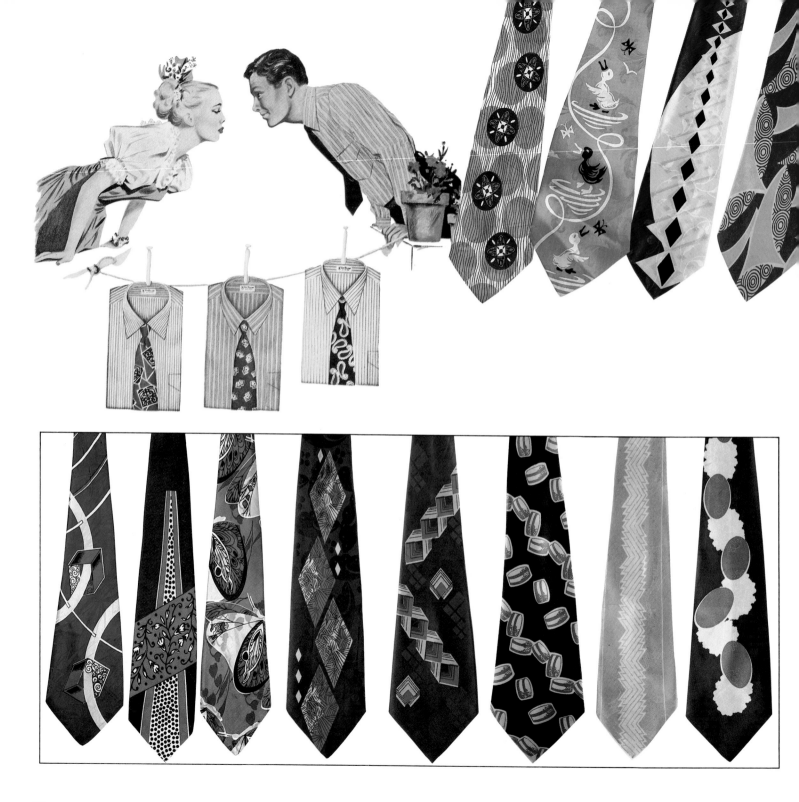

"When...have you heard of a man wearing out a tie? What counts is style, and today, with bold patterns, panels and new colors, we offer the consumer the widest selection in tie history."
—Allan Herbert of Bachrach (1948)

"The Vertical Look is a smart, modern look; a graceful sweep down your tie gives an effect that is as striking as it is fashionable."—McCurrach tie ad, *Apparel Arts*, October 1946

ADVER-TIES-ING

Season after season, it's the number one gift item for sales.
—*The Saturday Evening Post*, 1946

If the average man were to survey the contents of his closet, chances are he would find that most of his ties had been given to him by the women in his life. Forty years ago most ties were priced between $1.50 and $5.00, so a man could buy several at a time. The new working woman could afford to pamper her man, and, according to a 1949 article, it was women who bought 80 percent of the ties sold in department stores and 60 percent of those sold in specialty shops. While some women concerned themselves with practical features such as tie construction and fabric, nearly 90 percent of all ties were bought on impulse. The "Ham and Eggs" style probably survived only because it appealed to women, but even so it never represented more than 15 percent of tie sales at its peak. Throughout the '40s, the majority of men still favored conservative neckwear.

Neckwear advertising and sales were overwhelmingly seasonal and based on gift-giving. One of the most successful 1948 campaigns was launched by the Men's Tie Foundation (formerly Institute) to increase normally slack sales on Valentine's Day. Free charts, one entitled "How to Tie Your Boyfriend's Tie" and another for matching a tie to a boyfriend's complexion, were given away. The local tie-ins were contests to choose a "Miss Valen-tie." Father's Day was, of course, a crucial holiday for tie sales, as the Cohama company indicated in its 1950 text for "A Striking Promotion!": "Cohama puts fire into Father's Day neckwear selling with an unmatched ad 'For a Matchless Dad.'"

These ties were walking billboards, and frequently corporate and visual calling cards.

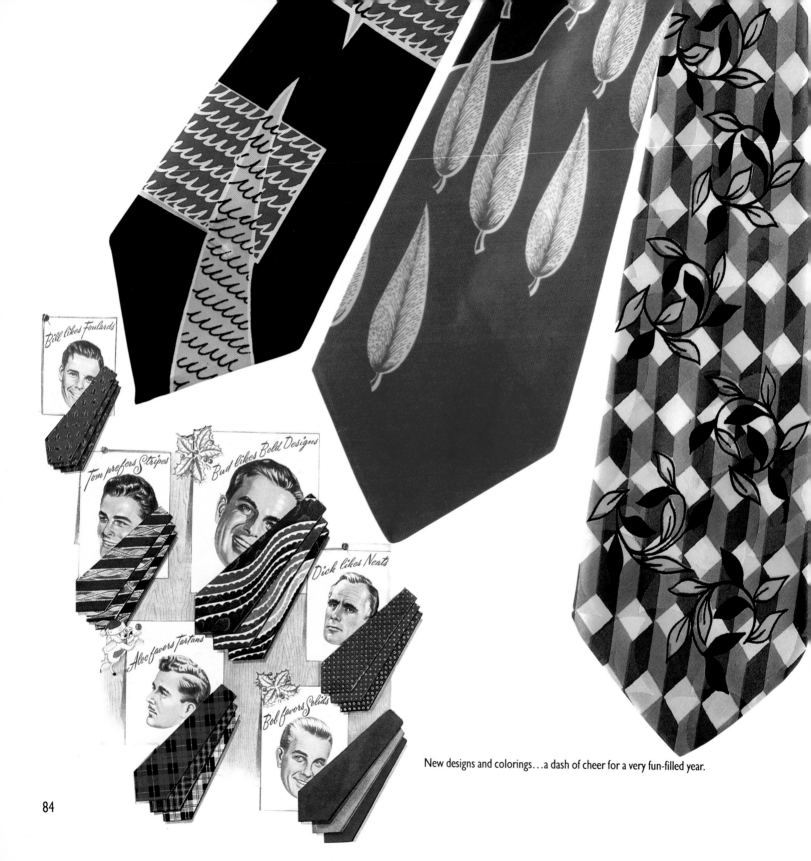

Bill likes Foulards

Tom prefers Stripes

Bud likes Bold Designs

Dick likes Neats

Alec favors Tartans

Bob favors Solids

New designs and colorings…a dash of cheer for a very fun-filled year.

84

CHENEY
makes many a merry Christmas!

Ties designed with assorted leaves and vivid flowers blossomed during the '40s. Their rich colors made them easy to "petal."

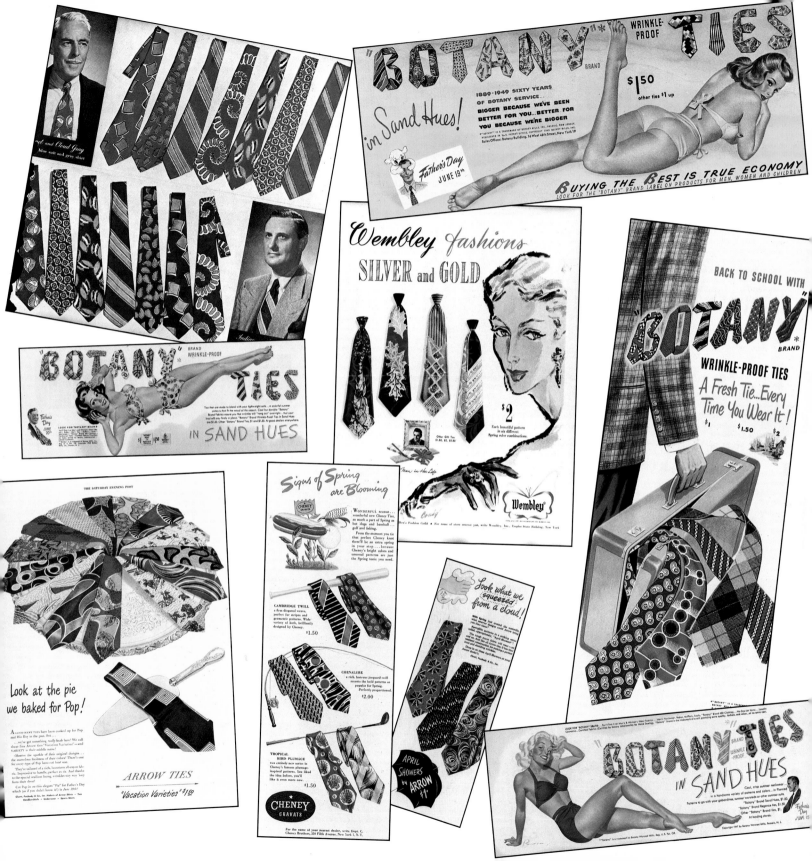

Let's go bowling, play ball, and get away from it all.

Tie-Died—The Forties Tie Goes Underground

In the Midwest, coin shaped figures, controlled patterns are the best sellers. In the South, bolder patterns, lots of colors. In the West, odd combinations, while the Northwest likes California types and darker colors. The East has already taken back conservative tie styles.
—*Apparel Arts* sales report, 1948

The end of the '40s tie era reflected the collapse of the post–World War II boom and the ensuing conservative mood in America. Several factors contributed to this change: a recession in the late '40s and early '50s, a prolonged Cold War, a hot Korean War, the specter of atomic warfare, and the rampant Red Scare paranoia. The general mood of growing conservatism included men's clothing: lapels grew narrower and colors became more somber. "Mister T," *Apparel Arts'* 1951 creation, personified this conservative trend and helped put an end to the "Bold Look." According to *Esquire,* the "Mister T" look meant "tapered crown hats, narrow brims, narrower shoulders, straight hanging lines, tapered trousers, less bulky shoes, pinpoint collars and small-knot ties."

English styling reemerged in American men's fashion with the 1949 abolition of clothes rationing in Britain. At the same time, moving to suburbia and fashion conformity were in full swing. Solids and striped ties were now just as popular as before the war, and these conservative items better matched the pastel and colored shirts coming into vogue. By 1951, the four-in-hand tie had slimmed down to 3½ inches wide, and college men liked their ties even slimmer. The postwar exuberance in men's ties had vanished. For the next fifteen years, conservatism in men's clothing was the dominant note.

The ties of the '40s are timeless examples of a unique American viewpoint. They display the individualism, informality, and humor that mirrored the optimism of the postwar era. Today this forgotten neckwear is being rediscovered by another generation of men. The "Ham and Eggs," the "Chest Warmer," and the "Christmas Dog" live again.

The "Chest Stripe" Tie, introduced about the same time and representative of the "Bold Look" style, was specifically designed to "tone down some of the bright neckwear that has been seen lately."–Tie Style Report, *Esquire,* April 1946. Chest Stripe's late appearance accurately reflects a more conservative attitude and, not unexpected, its persistence as a motif well into the late '50s.

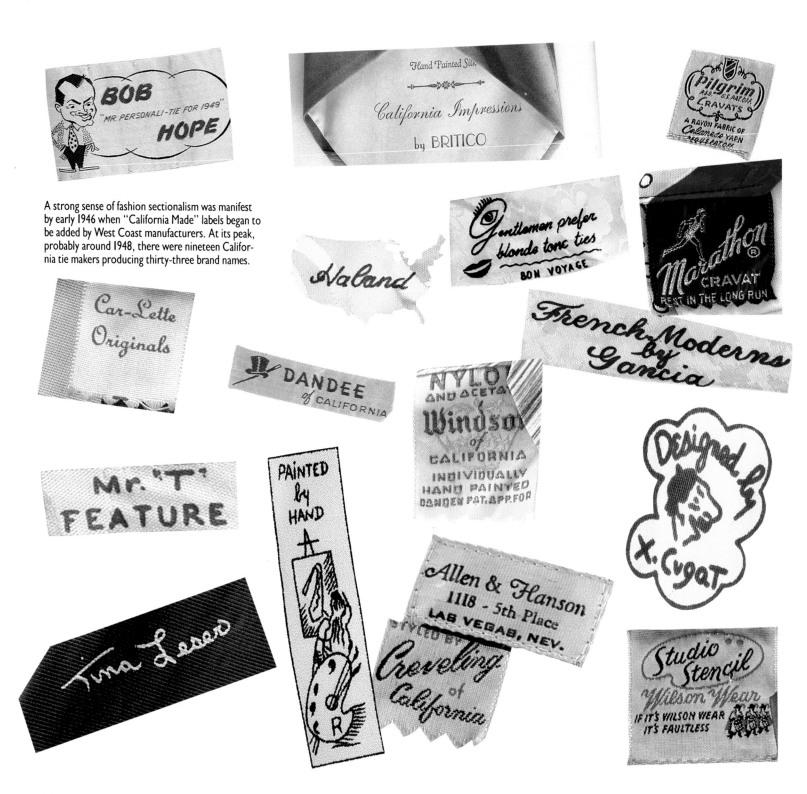

A strong sense of fashion sectionalism was manifest by early 1946 when "California Made" labels began to be added by West Coast manufacturers. At its peak, probably around 1948, there were nineteen California tie makers producing thirty-three brand names.

Acknowledgments

This book would not have been completed without the help of Marie, Nicholas, and Marcia Spark.

We would like to thank the following individuals for their assistance in gathering information and for lending their tie collections to be photographed for this book:

H. Thomas Steele, Jim Heimann, Carey Weiss, Harry Anderson, Tom Foden, Frans Evenhuis, Brad Benedict, Harry Kipper, Dr. Stanley Frileck, Yasu Yamada, Ron Olson, Parke Meek of Jadis, Los Angeles; Clive Piercy, Bill Murphy, Ed Smith, William Lasken, Don Frank, Kerrie Quinn, Walter Wanger, Norman Moore, Paul Glynn of Cowboys and Poodles, Jones, Jeff Stein Collection, How Sweet It Was, Tucson; Jerry & Susan Browstein of The Junk Store, Los Angeles; Bill & Jean Gold of Repeat Performance, Los Angeles; Brenda Cain, Will Hinds, Jim Leach of Western Costume, Los Angeles; Mark Werts & Tamara Nichols of the American Rag Cie, Los Angeles; Maddie & David of Thanks for the Memories, Los Angeles; Tommy Perse of Maxfield, Los Angeles; Karl Holm & Michael Alvidres of Paleeze, Los Angeles. Walton Rawls, our editor, remained unruffled through all our revisions.

In addition we would like to thank Myron Ackerman, former chairman of the Men's Tie Foundation, and Jerry Andersen, executive director of the Neckwear Association of America, who supplied us with oral and written history about the '40s tie industry, and the following tie manufacturers for granting us permission to use examples of their advertising of the period: James Morske, The Arrow Company; Laurence P. Stuart, Wembley Industries, Inc; Michael Rappaport, Damon Creations, Inc; Rose Ann De Marinis, Cheney Brothers, Inc; Manhattan, Van Heusen, Pulitzer, Regal Ties, Botany, Cohama Ties, Signet, McCurrach, Wilson Brothers.

Finally, a bow must go to the thousands of men who did not spill soup on their ties in the '40s and the tens of thousands of women who bought the "ties for their guys."

About the Authors

Rod Dyer is president and creative director of one of the leading graphic design and advertising firms in Los Angeles. Born in Pretoria, South Africa, Mr. Dyer worked in the advertising industry in that country before emigrating to America in 1958. As a designer Mr. Dyer has pursued myriad other interests, including interior and industrial design and the direction of several music videos.

Ron Spark practices medicine as a pathologist at Tucson Medical Center. His personal tie collection numbers more than 2000. He is also writer–moderator of a local Tucson medical TV program. Spark and his wife, Marcia, are American folk art collectors and have written and lectured extensively on antique patchwork quilts.

Steve Sakai is a Los Angeles-based photographer who was trained at Art Center College of Design in Pasadena, California. In 1980 he opened his own studio and currently does work for numerous national and international companies.

Ron Spark   Steve Sakai   Rod Dyer

Art Direction: Rod Dyer, Dyer/Kahn, Inc.
Design : Pam Bennett
        Margaret Miyuki
Photography: Steve Sakai
        Kathy Van Tassel,
        Steve Sakai / Photography